Travellers' Guide to the Italian Menu

Travellers' Guide to the
Italian
MENU

Absolute Press

Published by
Absolute Press (Publishers)
14 Widcombe Crescent, Bath, Avon. BA2 6AH.

© Absolute Press (Publishers)

First published 1985

Edited and Compiled by **Gill Rowley**

Illustrations Carl Willson

Cover printed by
Kennet & Avon Printing Company Limited,
26 Brock Street, Bath.

Text photoset and printed by
Photobooks (Bristol) Limited,
Barton Manor, St. Philips, Bristol.

Bound by W.H. Ware & Son Limited,
Tweed Road Industrial Estate,
Clevedon, Avon.

ISBN 0 948230 00 2

Contents

TRENTIN O-A
ADIGE
SWITZERLAND
Bolza
Aosta
Trento
Lake Como
Como
VAL
D'AOSTA
LOMBARDY
MILAN
Verona
TURIN
Mantua
PIEDMONT
Parma
BOLOG
FRANCE
GENOA
Modena
LIGURIA
Portofino
Sta Margherita
La Spezia
Portovenere
Viareggio
Lucca
San Remo
Pisa
Livorno
Arno
TUSCA
Elba
Civitaveo

AUSTRIA

LI-VENEZIA
GIULIA
Udine •
ETO   TRIESTE   YUGOSLAVIA
ENICE
Ja
EMILIA-
ROMAGNA

avenna

Rimini
• Pesaro
RINO
zo   • Ancona
THE
MARCHES
erugia
BRIA   *ADRIATIC SEA*
eto

• Pescara
ABRUZZO
MOLISE
ROME
LAZIO Campobasso •
• Foggia
CAMPANIA   Bari
Ischia • NAPLES   •
assari   PUGLIA   Brindisi
hero   • Potenza   •
Capri   Taranto •
BASILICATA

RDINIA

TYRRHENIAN SEA   CALABRIA
•
CAGLIARI   *Lipari*   Cantanzaro
Islands
IONIAN SEA
pani • PALERMO Messina •
• REGGIO DI CALABRIA
arsala
SICILY
• Agrigento   • Catania
• Syracuse

MEDITERRANEAN SEA

Introduction

Land of *pasta* and *pizza*, *risotto* and *ragù*, Italy has so many seemingly familiar dishes, cheerfully taken over and reproduced by expatriate Italians and non-Italians alike far from their native soil. Yet nothing can compare with eating Italian food in Italy, where no region can ever adopt a dish without providing its own distinctive hallmark – a herb typical of that region, a splash of the local wine, or a sprinkling of home-produced cheese. Even when you think you know exactly what to expect of a particular dish, a new locality will produce a fresh version.

Pasta is of course the regional food *par excellence*: every region has its own speciality, and sometimes its own name for a common type (for example, the Emilians call ribbon noodles *fettucine*, which are known elsewhere as *tagliatelle*). If you like *pasta*, you will be pretty safe with anything that appears under that heading on the restaurant menu, because a long, unfamiliar name is likely to denote a fanciful, locally-devised shape rather than the inclusion of any unfamiliar ingredients.

Pasta is certainly Italy's favourite food, and many Italians eat it twice a day without a thought to their waistlines: what is more, they regard it as a mere prelude to the main course of the meal. Even Christmas lunch is incomplete without *pasta*, as far as many Italians are concerned. And of course it is always better for being *fatta in casa* – home-made: there is simply no comparison between the rather dried-out, tired-tasting stuff we usually buy from the supermarkets and the freshly made version, wherever you happen to be eating it.

The real home of the *pizza* is Naples, but you will find it throughout the country, and indeed, if you do not want to indulge in a full-scale meal it makes the ideal lunchtime standby. Failing *pizza*, do not forget the wonderful country cheeses and delicatessen-type sausages, including the well-known *mortadella* and *salami*, which can sometimes be easier to track down than a restaurant that serves snacks.

But Italy is so much more than *pizza* and *pasta*. As with France, Italy's great strength lies in the range of its provincial cooking; from the spring lamb of Rome to the hearty mountain food of Umbria, fish from the Adriatic, pork from Emilia-Romagna, *risotto* from Milan, olives and figs from Calabria. This wealth of variety will provide the traveller with a constant source of pleasure.

Virtually all Italian restaurants are informal and usually very friendly – and if you have children, you need never worry that they will not be welcomed with open arms.

Buon appetito!

Phrases for the Restaurant

I want to reserve a table for . . . . . . at . . . . . .
Vorrei riservare un tavolo per . . . . . . alle . . . . . .
Have you a table for . . . . . .
Avete un tavolo per . . . . . .
A quiet table
Un posto tranquillo
A table near the window
Un tavolo vicino alla finestra
A table on the terrace
Un tavolo sulla terrazza
Could we have another table please?
Potremmo avere un altro tavolo, per favore?
I am in a hurry/we are in a hurry
Sono di fretta/Siamo di fretta
Please bring me the menu
Può darmi il menu, per favore
Can we have . . . . . . **please**
Possiamo avere un . . . . . . per favore
Local dishes
Piatti locali
How much is it?
Quanto costa?
What is it?
Che cos'è?
I did not order this
Non ho ordinato questo
Too much
Troppo, grazie
More
Ancòra, per favore
The bill please
Il conto per favore
Is service included?
È compreso il servizio?
I think there is a mistake in the bill
Penso che ci sia un errore nel conto
Do you accept travellers' cheques?
Accettate i traveller's cheques?

Restaurant Terms

antipasto
 ('before the meal'), starter, *hors d'oeuvre*
bicchiere
 glass
buongustai
 gourmets
caldo
 hot
cameriere
 waiter
conto
 bill
coperto
 cover (charge)
cena
 supper
colazione
 lunch
dente, al
 literally 'to the tooth', i.e. not over-cooked but still
 with a firm texture; a term used to describe the ideal
 point to which pasta, rice and certain vegetables
 should be cooked
dolci
 sweets, cakes and pastries
freddo
 cold
fresco
 fresh, cool
giorno, del
 (dish) of the day
menu
 menu

minestra, minestre
 first course, or soup course; soups
pasto
 meal
piatti
 dishes; *da farsi*, cooked to order; *del giorno*, of the
 day
pizzeria
 pizza restaurant
pranzo
 dinner
prezzo fisso
 fixed price
ristorante
 restaurant
tavola
 table; *calda*, 'hot table', restaurant primarily for
 quick lunches, taken standing or sitting
trattoria
 restaurant

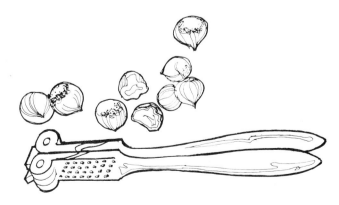

Menu Terms

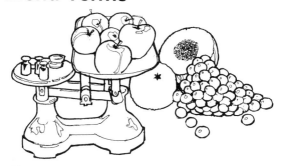

abbacchio

Roman dialect word for baby lamb, an Easter speciality of the region; often spit-roasted or cooked in the oven (*al forno*) with rosemary; *alla cacciatora* (hunter's-style), braised with olive oil, vinegar, sage, rosemary and garlic, and served with a sauce also including anchovies (celebrated Roman speciality); *brodettato*, cut into pieces with a sauce of olive oil, white wine, garlic, egg and lemon; *alla scottadito*, cutlets, grilled

acciuga, acciughe

anchovy, anchovies (see *alici*), common garnish for pizza; *carne ai capperi e*, veal with a sauce of capers, anchovies and herbs (Umbrian dish)

aceto

vinegar

affumicato

smoked

agliata, all'

in garlic sauce

aglio

garlic

agnello

lamb; *all'arrabbiata* ('angry'), cooked over a very high flame and sprinkled with salt, pepper and vinegar; *bistecchine fritte di*, fried chops; *e fagioli alla toscana*, Tuscan casserole of lamb and beans, with garlic and herbs; *in fricassea*, fricassee; *con sottaceti*, cooked with olive oil, white wine, rosemary, garlic and pickled vegetables; *trippato*, in egg sauce; *alla veneziana* (Venetian-style), cooked in milk; see also *abbacchio*

agnolotti

type of pasta, crescent-shaped, served with various

stuffings; *alla piemontese* (Piedmont-style), stuffed with minced veal and ham, cheese, egg and nutmeg

agoni
variety of shad, usually cooked in sage-flavoured butter

agrodolce
sweet-sour sauce, made of honey, sugar, vinegar and lemon juice

aguglie
garfish, green-boned species served either fried or stewed in a sauce of tomatoes, onions and oregano

albicocche
apricots

alici
anchovies; *al gratin*, fresh, oven-baked with breadcrumb topping; *all'ischiana* (Ischia-style), fresh, oven-baked with olive oil, lemon juice and wild marjoram

alla, al, all'
in the style of, or simply 'with'

allodole
larks

alloro
bay

amaretti
miniature macaroons, often served with the coffee after a meal

amatriciana
see *bucatini*

ananas
pineapple

anara
regional name for duck in the Veneto

anguilla
eel; *arrosta*, roast; *al girarrosto*, cooked on a spit; *risotto adriatico all'*, risotto with eels from the Adriatic (speciality of Ravenna); *in umido al vino*, stewed with wine, tomato purée and bay leaves; *alla valligiana* (in the style of the valley), split open and cooked in its own juices, sprinkled with pepper

animelle
sweetbreads

anitra
duck; *ripiena*, roast, and stuffed with its own liver, veal, bacon, Parmesan, breadcrumbs, egg and herbs; *alla salsa piccante*, in a piquant sauce; *alla valligiana* (in the style of the valley), stuffed with its own offal, bacon, herbs and onion and boiled

anolini
type of pasta, usually served stuffed with spinach or

with *stracotto*

antipasto

('before the meal'), starter, appetizer, *hors d'oeuvre*

anzio pie

see *pasticcio di maccheroni all'anziana*

aragosta

rock lobster, langouste or crayfish (not the true lobster, but the type most commonly found in the Mediterranean); *frittelle di*, lobster fritters, pieces fried in batter and served with mayonnaise

arancia, aranci

orange(s); *al caramel* (or *arranci caramellizzati*), sliced and served in caramelized juice; *ripiene*, filled with other fruit; *tagliati*, macerated slices of

arancine

balls of fried rice with chopped meat and *caciocavallo* cheese

arigusta

rock lobster, langouste or crayfish (see *aragosta*)

aringhe

herrings

àrista

loin of pork; *alla fiorentina* (Florence-style), slow-roasted with rosemary, garlic and clove; *di maiale arrosto*, roast; *perugina* (Perugia-style), roast pork with fennel

arrabbiata

'angry', usually denoting the use of strong flavourings or sometimes simply that the dish is cooked over a high flame

arrosto

roast

arrostito

grilled

arrotolato

stuffed

arselle

clams (Genoese and Sardinian name)

asciutta

dry (especially of pasta and pasta dishes)

asiago

sharp, granular mountain cheese made from partly skimmed cow's milk in the Veneto region

asparagi

asparagus; *alla fiorentina* (Florence-style), boiled, tossed in butter with Parmesan and seasoning, and topped with fried eggs; *punti di*, tips of

baccalà
dried, salted cod, also known as *stoccafisso*, stock-fish; *alla fiorentina* (Florence-style), with oil, garlic and pepper; *mantecata* ('worked'), creamed, with milk, oil and garlic; *alla veneziana* (Venetian-style), cooked with butter, milk and flour, onions and anchovy; *alla vicentina*, variant of the latter, from Vicenza

bagna cauda
hot cocktail dip or sauce made of anchovy and garlic

balsamella
béchamel (see *besciamella*)

banana
banana

barbabietola
beetroot

barbuta
brill

beccaccia
woodcock; *crostini di*, *arrosto*, roast woodcock on toast

beccaccino
snipe

basilico
basil

bel paese
('beautiful country'), mild, creamy cheese made in Lombardy

ben cotta
well cooked (of steak)

besciamella
béchamel sauce, basic mixture of flour, butter and milk which is essential to many pasta dishes, including *lasagne*

bianchetti
whitebait

bianco
white; used of sauces, in particular, to denote the absence of tomatoes; *in bianco*, boiled

biete
Swiss chard

bignè
deep-fried pastry puffs

bigoli
type of pasta, Venetian name for a sort of *cannelloni*; *coi rovinazzi*, with cockscombs and sage

birra
beer

bisati
eels

bistecca
beef or veal steak; *alla pizzaiola*, with tomato and garlic sauce; *alla fiorentina* (Florence-style), porterhouse, grilled over charcoal; see also *al sangue*, *a puntino* and *ben cotta*

bitto
country cheese from Lombardy made from a mixture of cow's and goat's milk

bocconcini
'mouth pleasers', see *olivette*

bollito
boiled (meat); *misto*, classic dish of various boiled meats and haricot beans, from Piedmont

bolognese
generally denoting a (meat-) gravy and tomato sauce

bombette
little 'bombs', or balls

bomboline del ricotta in brodo
soup with dumplings made of ricotta cheese

bombolini
doughnuts

bonnarelli
Roman name for thin ribbon pasta also known as *tagliolini*

bonito
a small tunny fish

bòsega
clams

bottarga
tuna eggs either toasted or seasoned with oil and lemon

bovolo
sea-snail

brace, alla
on the embers, grilled

braciole
thin slices of meat, usually rolled round a filling

braciolette
slices of veal wrapped round ham or other filling

bracioline
cutlets

branzino
sea bass

brasato
braised; *alla bresciana* (Brescia-style), beef braised in oil and red wine, with onions, garlic and bacon; *di*

manzo, braised beef

bresaola

dried salt beef, served thinly sliced as a starter with oil and lemon juice

broccoli

broccoli; *alla romana* (Roman-style), sautéed with garlic in white wine and olive oil; *alla siciliana* (Sicilian-style), cooked with red wine, olive oil, onion, olives, anchovies and Parmesan cheese

brodetto

('little broth'), rather liquid fish stew, or soup, from Ravenna, containing squid, red mullet, sea bass, eel and shellfish, tomatoes, herbs, usually some saffron, and garlic; possibly with slices of bread floating in it

brodo (ristretto)

clear soup or broth; *di cappone*, chicken consommé; *di manzo*, beef stock; *pasta in, con fegatini e fagioli/lenticchie/piselli*, pasta in chicken stock with chicken livers and haricot beans/lentils/peas

bucatini

type of pasta (also called *perciatelli*) resembling thick, hollow spaghetti; *all'amatriciana*, served with a sauce of tomatoes, bacon, chillis and *pecorino* cheese

buccellato

ring-shaped fruitcake, its centre filled with wine-marinated strawberries

budino

pudding, dessert; *di prugne*, flan filled with prunes and other dried fruits, nuts, lemon peel, Marsala and cream; *toscano* (Tuscan), baked cheese mould with almonds and dried fruit

bue

beef

burrida

Genoese name for *brodetto*

burrini

same as *buttiri*

burro

butter; *salsa di*, butter sauce made with wine, parsley and onion

busecca

highly seasoned veal tripe, served with beans (speciality of Lombardy region)

buttiri

a Calabrian version of the cheese *cacio a cavallo* which has fresh butter in its centre

cacciagione
game, venison

cacciatora, alla
hunter's-style, usually describing poultry, fish or game cooked in a simple sauce: e.g. braised with olive oil, white wine, herbs and vegetables (mushrooms, tomatoes, spring onions)

cacciucco (livornese)
fish stew (speciality of Leghorn, Livorno) containing octopus, squid, lobster and crab, white wine, tomato sauce and garlic (not unlike the *bouillabaisse* of southern France)

cacio a cavallo, caciocavallo
cheese of similar type to *provolone*

caciotta romana
semi-hard, sweet sheep's-milk cheese from Rome and its environs (Lazio or Latium region)

caciotto
general name for local cheese which is made from either cow's or sheep's milk in the Marches, from goat's milk in Capri, and from sheep's milk in Tuscany and Umbria

caffè
(*espresso*) coffee, black, strong and aromatic, served in a small cup; see also *cappucino*

caffelatte
coffee and hot milk in equal proportions

calamaretti
baby squid; *del Golfo fritte*, from the Bay of Biscay, deep-fried

calamari
squid; *fritti*, fried; *e piselli alla livornese*, Livorno-style, with peas; *in umido*, stewed in red wine

calzoni
(1) small egg pasta envelopes, like ravioli, usually filled with meat: (2) Neopolitan version of pizza, with the crust folded round the base like a turn-over

canestrato
Sicilian sheep's milk cheese

cannarozzetti
type of pasta, name used in the Abruzzi for *ditalini* or *tubetti* (short, ribbed pasta)

cannella
cinnamon

cannellini
dried haricot or kidney beans, served with an oil-and-vinegar dressing

cannelloni
 type of pasta, large tubes of noodle dough filled with a meat and béchamel mixture and baked

cannoli
 tubes of crisp pastry stuffed with ricotta cheese, candied fruit and chocolate, a Sicilian speciality

capelli d'angelo
 'angel hair', type of pasta; very fine noodles usually served in a meat broth with Parmesan cheese sprinkled over

capitone
 large eel

capòn
 capon; *alla canevera*, sewn into a pig's bladder with pieces of guinea-fowl and beef

caponata, caponatina (di melanzane or alla siciliana)
 Sicilian dish of cooked vegetables, based on sautéed aubergines and including tomatoes, celery, capers and olives, possibly with anchovy or anchovy juice (Catanian version); in Palermo seafood ingredients are added

capparozzoli
 clams

cappe
 clams

cappellacci
 type of pasta usually served stuffed with pumpkin (see *zucca*) and peculiar to Ferrara

cappelletti
 'little hats', type of pasta; dumplings stuffed with chicken, pork, *mortadella*, ricotta, Parmesan and nutmeg; *alla bolognese*, with gravy and tomato sauce

capperi
 capers

cappuccino
 coffee made with hot, foaming milk, and sometimes served sprinkled with finely grated chocolate

capretto
 kid, young goat; *alla cacciatora* (hunter's-style), cooked with onion and white wine; *ripieno al forno*, stuffed with herbs and roasted; *al vino bianco*, braised in white wine and Marsala, with herbs and vegetables

capriata
 purée of dried beans and olive oil served with green vegetables or pimentos, onion and tomato

capriolo
 roe-deer; *in umido*, venison stew; *alla valdostana*

(Val d'Aosta-style), cooked in white wine and brandy, with white truffles and cheese

carciofi

globe artichokes; *alla crema*, in a cream sauce; *alla giudia* (Jewish-style), young whole artichokes, deep-fried, usually with parsley and garlic (Roman speciality); *di insalata*, sliced with lemon juice and oil; *alla manticiana*, grilled; *ripieni,* filled with anchovies, garlic and breadcrumbs and braised in wine; *alla romana* (Roman-style), young whole artichokes casseroled with meat and garlic; *alla veneziana* (Venetian style), braised in oil and white wine

cardi

chards; *alla bagna cauda*, Piedmontese dish with a hot sauce including shredded garlic, anchovies, cream and truffles

carne

meat; sometimes denotes veal (see *acciughe*)

carote

carrots

carpione

carp

carrozza, in

'in a carriage': Neapolitan term applying especially to fried mozzarella cheese sandwiches

carte di giuoco

('card-game'), type of pasta, irregularly shaped, served with tomato and sometimes mutton and also known as *stracci*

cartoccio

oiled paper case, or tinfoil, in which food is cooked

casalinga, (alla)

homemade, home-style

casereccio

homemade

cassata

ice-cream dish in which a shell of cream or chocolate encases lighter ice-cream; *(alla) siciliana*, Sicilian sponge-cage frosted with chocolate and containing ricotta, mixed candied fruit and, frequently, ice-cream

castagne

chestnuts; *al marsala*, cooked in marsala and red wine with sugar and served either hot or cold with cream

cavolfiori

cauliflower; *saltati al burro e aglio*, sautéed in butter with garlic

cavoli-cappucci
  brussels sprouts; *agrodolci*, with sweet and sour sauce
cavolini di Bruxelles
  Brussels sprouts
cavolirape
  kohl rabi
cavolo
  cabbage
cazzuola
  stew; *di montone alla fiorentina*, of mutton, Florence-style, with pig-meat, beans or pasta, tomato sauce and vegetables, with a fried-breadcrumb topping
ceci
  chick peas; *e castagne*, with roasted chestnuts; *di Navelli*, on fried bread with a sauce of olive oil, onion and rosemary
cedro
  citron
cee
  baby eels; *alla viareggina* (Viareggio-style), with tomatoes, garlic, herbs and wine
cefalo
  grey mullet, usually served roasted or grilled
cenci alla fiorentina
  crisp-fried sweet pastries
cervella, cervelli
  (calves') brains; *al burro nero*, in black butter; *dorate alla milanese* (Milan-style), in egg and breadcrumbs, fried
cervellada
  sausage made from pork fat, cheese, marrow, and spices
cervo
  venison; *con salsa di ciliegie*, with cherry sauce
cetrioli
  cucumbers
chiodi di girofano
  cloves
cicoria
  chicory
cieche
  elvers (young eels), served in Pisa cooked in oil with sage
ciliegii
  cherries
cima
  breast (of animal); also, particularly, cold stuffed veal

(*di vitello*), a popular dish of Genoa, sometimes so described (*alla genovese*), the stuffing consisting of veal offal and leg meat, eggs, artichokes, Parmesan cheese and peas; it can be bought by weight in *rosticcerie* (cooked-food shops)

cinghiale
wild boar; *in agrodolce*, with sweet-sour sauce; *arrosto*, roast; *alla cacciatora*, (hunter's-style), braised in white wine and stock with vegetables; *stufato di*, stew

cioccolato
chocolate; *budino*, or *spuma di*, mousse

cipolle
onions

cipolline
chives, shallots, spring onions; *in agrodolce*, tiny spring onions in thin sweet-sour tomato sauce

cocciule
clams (Sardinia)

cocomero
watermelon

coda
tail; *di bue alla vaccinara*, oxtail, butcher's-style (Roman speciality, braised with wine and vegetables)

conchiglia
small shellfish

conchiglie
type of pasta resembling sea-shells

condito
seasoned, tasty

coniglio
rabbit; *bollito al sale aromatico*, stewed with herbs, lemon and garlic; *fritto dorato*, marinated, coated in egg and flour and fried; *alla livornese* (Livorno-style), sautéed in tomato sauce with garlic, onion and anchovy; *alla portoghese* (Portuguese style), stewed with vegetables

consomme all'uova
beef consommé poured over mixture of lemon juice and beaten eggs, sprinkled with grated cheese

contorni
vegetables served to accompany or garnish a main course

coppa
(1) in Rome, brawn made from pig's head: (2) in the Veneto, a meat loaf made with layers of ham, tongue and *mortadella*

coratella
offal, e.g. hearts, lungs, liver, kidney

coscetto
leg (often, of lamb)

coscia
leg

cosciotti, cosciotto
legs, leg; *di rane fritte*, deep-fried frog's legs

costa
rib, chop

costata
fillet steak or rib chop; *alla fiorentina* (Florence-style), grilled fillet of veal cooked with oil and seasoning; *alla pizzaiola*, with tomatoes, garlic and wild marjoram (Campania)

costolette
cutlets, chops (same as *cotolette*); *di agnello alla marinetti*, lamb, braised in white wine with herbs; *alla bolognese* (Bologna-style), veal cutlet, coated in egg, topped with a slice of ham and melted cheese; *di maiale*, pork chops; *(di vitello) alla milanese*, breaded veal cutlet (a rib chop), Milan-style, cooked in butter and garnished with lemon and parsley; *di vitello alla valdostana* (Val d'Aosta-style), sautéed veal, stuffed with *fontina* cheese

costolettine
small chops; *di agnello fritte*, lamb rib chops fried in Parmesan cheese batter

cotechino
highly spiced sausage made from pork (Roman speciality); *con fagioli*, boiled, with (haricot) beans; *con lenticchie*, with lentils (New Year dish)

cotolette
see *costolette*

cotolettine
see *costolettine*

cotto
cooked, done; *a puntino*, just to the right amount (of steak, medium rare)

cozze
mussels; *alla marinara* (sailor-style), marinated in white wine and oil; *al vino bianco*, cooked in white wine with garlic and parsley and served cold

crema
custard or cream; *caramella*, crème caramel; *di piselli (di pollo, di pomodoro)* cream of pea (chicken, tomato) soup

crescione
watercress

crespelle
pancakes; served in Lombardy wrapped round chopped meat and served with a cheese sauce

crespolini
thin pancakes, served filled with Parmesan and cream cheese, spinach and chicken livers, with a topping of Parmesan and mozzarella cheese and béchamel sauce

crocchette
croquettes; *di cervella*, made with calf's brain, pounded into a paste, dipped into egg and flour and fried in butter

crostacei
shellfish

crosta (di torta), crostata, crostatina
(pie-)crust, tart; *crostata alla napoletana* (Naples-style), chocolate cream pie with apricots; *di ricotta*, cheesecake; *alla siciliana* (Sicilian-style), open pie containing creamy filling with orange and lemon peel and chopped pistachio nuts

crostini
croûtons, or small cubes of fried bread, often spread with cheese; *di fegatini*, with chopped chicken livers and ham; *alla provatura*, dipped in egg and baked with a piece of buffalo-milk cheese (*provatura* or mozzarella) on top

crudo
raw

cupete
soft pastries made with honey, sugar and walnuts

cuscusu
couscous, speciality of Sicily

datteri
dates; *di mare*, shellfish, or 'sea dates', particular kind of delicate-flavoured Mediterranean shellfish found off Genoese coast and used in soups

dentice
dentex, type of fish found in Mediterranean waters, usually served grilled or roasted

diavola, alla
devilled, often denoting the inclusion of chillis or other hot flavours in the sauce

disossato
boned

dolce sardo
soft cheese from Sardinia

dolci
desserts, sweets, cakes; *dolce mafarka*, rice mould flavoured with coffee, lemon and orange-flower water

dorato
gilded, golden brown

dragoncello
tarragon

endivia
see *indivia*

erbe
herbs

erbette
greens

escaloppe
escalopes; *alla milanese*, fried veal, with parsley and lemon

escarole
Batavian endive

espresso
see *caffè*

fagiano
pheasant; *arrosto*, roast; *con funghi e besciamella*, with mushrooms and béchamel sauce; *con crema e tartufi*, with cream and truffles

fagioli

dried kidney beans or haricots; *alla fiorentina* (Florence-style), with oil, herbs and onions; *minestrone di*, in soup with celery and tomatoes, Tuscan speciality; *in salsa*, salad of boiled beans eaten cold with anchovies and an oil-and-vinegar dressing

fagiolini

French, or string, beans; *col tonno*, with tuna fish

fagottini

bundles; *di vitello leccabaffi*, veal, with anchovies and cheese

farcito

stuffed

farfalle

('butterflies'), type of pasta, so-called because of their shape, sometimes served with a sauce of *prosciutto* and tomato

farfalline

('little butterflies'), type of pasta, containing egg, in the shape of a butterfly

farina

flour

farinacei

farinaceous (cereal) dishes

fave

broad beans

fegato

liver; *alla veneziana* (Venetian style), calf's, with onions

fegatelli

liver; *di maiale alla toscana*, pork (Tuscan-style), either spit-roasted or fried with breadcrumbs, Parmesan and herbs with olive oil and red wine

fegatini (di pollo)

chicken livers

feraona

guinea-fowl

ferri, ai

('on the irons'), grilled

fetta, fettina

slice, little (or thin) slice

fettucine

egg noodles, type of pasta; name used in Emilia region for *tagliatelle* (ribbon noodles or strip macaroni); *al burro*, with butter (Roman speciality); *al doppio burro*, or *all'Alfredo*, tossed in butter, cream and Parmesan cheese; *alla marinara* (sailor-style),

Neapolitan dish with fresh tomato sauce and basil; *all'uovo*, buttered egg noodles

fichi

figs; celebrated in Sicily, commonly included in fruit salads and sometimes eaten with Parma ham; *d'India* ('Indian figs'), prickly pears, eaten throughout southern Italy

filetto

fillet

finanziera di pollo

chicken livers, mushrooms, sweetbreads and truffles in a meat and tomato sauce, presented in a pastry shell (Piedmontese speciality)

finocchi

fennel; *al burro e formaggio*, sautéed, with butter and Parmesan; *fritti*, fried; *all' olio*, braised in olive oil

fiorentina, alla

Florence-style, often alluding to the inclusion of spinach

fiorentina, la

grilled steak, Florence-style: T-bone steak flavoured with crushed peppercorns

focaccia

Genoese name for pizza

foiolo

tripe

fondi (di carciofo)

(artichoke) hearts

fonduta

Piedmontese dish of melted (*fontina*) cheese with milk, eggs and sometimes grated white truffles, a speciality of Piedmont; *alla parmigiana*, made from alternative layers of sliced Parmesan, white truffles and grated Parmesan, melted in the oven

fontina

Piedmontese cheese, like a fat, creamy gruyère, used in *fonduta*; true *fontina* comes from the Val d'Aosta region

formaggio

cheese; *di grana*, Parmesan

forno, al

in the oven, oven-baked

fragole, fragoline

strawberries; *di bosco, dei boschi*, wood (wild); *di mare*, sea strawberries or baby squid (same as *moscardini* and *polpetti*)

freddo

cold

fresco
uncooked, raw

fricassea
fricassee

frittata
omelette; *affogata* ('drowned'), omelette steeped in tomato sauce, a Tuscan speciality; *al formaggio*, cheese; *genovese*, Genoese, with spinach

frittatina
small omelette or pancake; *di cipolle*, onion omelette; *imbottita*, stuffed pancakes, with a filling (e.g. of cheese or cheese and spinach)

frittelle
pastry puffs or fritters, filled with cheese, shellfish or other items and served deep-fried and very hot; *di San Giuseppe* (speciality for St Joseph's Day), rice fritters made with lemon and orange peel and marsala

fritto, fritte
fried (e.g. potatoes, *patate fritte*)

fritto misto
mixed fry or grill; *di mare*, fish

frittura mista
mixed fry or grill (Milanese name for *fritto misto*)

frutta
fruit; *candita*, candied, speciality of Sicily; *cotta*, stewed; *insalata di*, salad; *di mare*, seafood, assorted shellfish; *di stagione*, of the season

funghi
mushrooms; *fritti*, fried, in batter; *alla genovese* (Genoa-style), sprinkled with pepper, cooked in olive oil on grape leaves and eaten with cloves; *alla graticola*, grilled; *ripieni*, stuffed, with Parmesan, bacon or ham, garlic, herbs and, optionally, breadcrumbs; *stufati* ('smothered'), in tomatoes, garlic and herbs; *trifolati*, sautéed, with garlic and parsley; *in umido*, stewed, in olive oil with garlic and mint

galantina
boned meat, game, poultry or fish, stuffed and served cold

gallina
hen

gamberi
shrimps, large prawns; *dorati*, fried in batter; *di fiume* (river), crayfish

gamberetti
prawns
gambero di mare
true lobster, rarely found in Mediterranean waters (see *aragosta*)
gamberoni
large sea prawns of the Genoese coast
garganelli
(From a verb meaning 'to gulp down'), type of homemade egg pasta, quill-shaped with ridged surface, speciality of Romagna served with *ragu* or a sauce of cream and *prosciutto*
gasse
type of pasta in the shape of bows, served with *pesto* or in broth on the Italian Riviera
gelato
ice-cream; *di albicocche*, apricot; *di banana al rum*, flavoured with banana and rum; *di caffe*, coffee; *di cioccolata*, chocolate; *di fragole*, strawberry; *di nocciola*, hazelnut; *di torrone*, nougat
genovese, alla
Genoa-style, sometimes denoting the presence of fish
ghiaccio, ghiacciato
ice, iced
gioddù
Sardinian yoghurt
girarrosto, al
spit-roasted
girato (al fuoco di legna)
spit-roasted (over wood fire); *misto*, mixed spit-roast, with different meats such as poultry, pork and sausage
gnocchetti
miniature dumplings, type of pasta; *cacio e ova*, cheese and egg, also containing pieces of bacon (known colloquially as *strangolapreti*)
gnocchi
small dumplings, type of pasta; *del casentino*, made with spinach and ricotta; *di parmigiana*, made with Parmesan and served as an appetizer; *di patate*, made from potatoes and flour; *col pesto*, with *pesto* sauce; *alla piemontese*, (Piedmont-style), served with a brown sauce and Parmesan cheese; *di polenta*, made of yellow maize flour; *di ricotta*, made from *ricotta* cheese and flour; *alla romana* (Roman-style), semolina dumplings, cooked in tomato sauce, topped with cheese and placed under the grill; *verdi*,

made from spinach and ricotta cheese (northern Italian speciality)

gorgonzola
strong, mellow, blue-veined cow's-milk cheese from Lombardy region

gramigna
type of egg pasta, short and curled, served with a sauce containing cream and sausage (speciality of the Emilia-Romagna region)

grana
(1) grain: (2) hard, coarse-textured cheese (particularly Parmesan)

granceole, grancevole
large Adriatic spider-crabs, bright red in colour

granchio
crab

granite
flavoured water-ices with the texture of shaved ice, not usually served as a dessert but eaten as a refreshment in cafés; *al caffè*, coffee; *di fragole*, strawberry; *di limone*, lemon; *con panna*, with whipped cream

granoturco
sweetcorn

granseole veneziane
Venetian dish of local variety of crab

grappa
brandy made by fermented grape skins and pips that remain after juice has been drawn off

gremolata, gremolada
mixture of chopped parsley, garlic and lemon peel traditionally served with *osso bucco*

griglia, alla
grilled

grissini
bread sticks (originally from Turin)

groviera
Italian gruyère

gropetti
slices of veal wrapped round ham or other stuffing

imbottito
stuffed

impanato
breaded

indivia
  endive
insalata
  salad; *di frutta*, fruit; *verde*, green; *mista*, mixed; *di pomodoro*, tomato
involtini
  slices of veal wrapped round ham or other stuffing

lampone
  raspberries
lardo
  salt pork; *affumicato*, bacon
lasagne
  type of pasta, thin slices of pasta cooked in the oven (*al forno*) with a béchamel sauce, a meat and tomato sauce, and cheese; *alla piemontese*, with the addition of white truffles; *verde*, same pasta made with spinach, cooked in a similar fashion
latte
  milk; *maiale al*, pork cooked in milk; *patate al*, potatoes cooked in milk, but not mashed; *pollo al*, chicken cooked in milk
lattemiele
  whipped cream, speciality of Milan
latticini
  fresh mountain cheeses
lattuga
  lettuce; *ripiena* ('stuffed'), cooked in beef consommé and served with gravy, Easter speciality of La Spezia
lattume
  soft tuna roe
lauro
  bay (leaf, leaves)
legumi
  vegetables

lenticchie
lentils; *in umido*, stewed, with onion, garlic, mint
and olive oil

lepre
hare; *in agrodolce*, in sweet-sour sauce; *arrosto di,
con senape e brandy*, roast, with mustard and
brandy; *alla cacciatora* (hunter's-style), cooked in a
sauce of oil, sage, garlic and rosemary; *alla montana*,
or *alla montanura*, mountain-style, casseroled with
red wine, pine kernels, sultanas, sugar and cinnamon;
in salmi, pot-roasted and served in a sauce containing wine and its own liver; *in umido*, stewed; *alla
veneta*, cooked on the spit (Paduan speciality)

lesso, lesse
boiled (e.g. potatoes, *patate lesse*)

limone
lemon

lingua
tongue; *di bue*, ox; *in salsa*, served in a sauce of
white wine, chopped anchovy and capers

linguine
type of pasta, like thin, flat spaghetti, usually eaten
with meat sauce; *alla romana* (Roman-style), cooked
in butter with ricotta cheese

livornese, alla
Livorno-style, usually with fish, garlic, tomato and
parsley

lonza
cured fillet of pork, flavoured with wine, spices and
garlic, cut in thin slices and served raw as a starter

luganega, luganica
a long, curling, sweet sausage

lumache
snails; *in zimino*, stewed in oil with onion, garlic,
mushrooms and herbs

maccaroncelli
type of pasta, like thick, tubular spaghetti

maccheroni
macaroni, type of pasta, in thick tubes; *alla chitarra*,
cut into strips on the wires of a guitar- (*chitarra-*)
shaped utensil (speciality of Abruzzi region); *al forno*,
cooked in the oven with tomatoes, mushrooms,
cheese and a white sauce; *con gamberi*, with
shrimps (Pescaran speciality); *alla marinara* (sailor-

style), with tomato sauce; *alla napoletana* (Naples-style), with tomatoes and basil; *pasticcio di, all'anziana*, Anzio macaroni pie (see *pasticcio*), *alle vongole*, with a clam and tomato sauce

macedonia di frutta
fruit salad

maggiorana
marjoram

magro
lean

maiale
pork; *arrosto di, all'alloro*, roast, with bay leaves; *arrosto di, al latte*, cooked in milk; *bistecche di*, chops; *costa di, alla griglia*, marinated pork chops, cooked under the grill; *fegatelli di, alla toscana*, liver, Tuscan-style, either spit-roasted or fried with bread-crumbs, parmesan and herbs with olive oil and red wine; *ubriaco* ('drunken'), in red wine

maionese
mayonnaise (made only with oil, eggs and lemon juice)

maltagliati
('badly cut') type of short pasta used for soups, especially soups that include beans or chick peas

mandorle
almonds

manicotti
type of pasta, large tubes served stuffed and baked with a sauce

mantecato
worked, creamed

manzo
beef; *bollito*, boiled; *alla bresciana* (Brescia-style), casseroled with salt pork, garlic, butter and red wine; *brodo di*, consommé; *costa di, al vino rosso*, rib of, marinated in red wine; *fettine di, alla sorrentina*, thin steaks Sorrento-style, with tomatoes and olives; *alla lombarda* (Lombardy-style), braised, then cooked with parsley, carrots, onions and celery in red wine; *ripieno arrosto*, stuffed roast; *stufato di, alla genovese*, Genoese beef stew

marasca
morello cherry

maraschino
liqueur brandy made from cherries

mare, al
sea-style, denoting the inclusion of seafood

marinara, alla
sailor-style; southern Italian sauce with tomato, oregano, oil and garlic

marinato
marinated

maritozzi (romani)
small soft buns made with egg dough and raisins (Lenten speciality in Rome area)

marsala
dark, strong, amber-coloured and semi-sweet Sicilian wine, not unlike a heavy sherry

masanète
clams

mascarpone, mascherpone
small fresh double-cream cheeses marketed in individual muslin-wrapped cylinders; *crema di*, served with fruit or sugar, or sugar and maraschino, or with powdered chocolate; alternatively, sometimes eaten with liqueurs

mazzacuogni, mazzancolle
very large prawns, like scampi

mela
apple

melanzane
aubergines; *funghetti*, sautéed in small pieces, with skin left on; *alla parmigiana*, baked with Parmesan and mozzarella cheese; *ripiene*, stuffed, with anchovy fillets, olives, garlic, capers, parsley and bread

melone
melon

menta
mint

merluzzo
cod

messicani (di vitello) con risotto
('Mexicans with risotto'), rolls of veal stuffed with meat, cheese, bread, garlic, spices and egg, cooked in wine or spit-roasted and basted with wine

miele
honey

migliaccio
cake made of chestnut flour to accompany *uccelletti*, small birds

mille foglie
('Thousand leaves', cf. French *mille feuilles*), flaky pastry

minestra, minestre
soup or pasta course; thick vegetable soup; *torinese*,

vegetable soup with saffron and garlic

minestrone

thick vegetable soup (literally 'big soup'), sometimes
including rice and usually sprinkled with Parmesan
cheese; *alla genovese*, with *pesto*; *alla milanese*,
with green vegetables, rice and bacon

misto

mixed

mitili

mussels

monte bianco

'white mountain', dessert made with puréed chestnut and chocolate, rum, sugar and cream

montone

mutton

morbido

soft, tender

morene

lampreys or sea-eels

mortadella

large, spiced pork sausage, speciality of Bologna

moscardini

sea strawberries or baby squid (same as *fragoline di
mare* and *polpetti*)

mostarda

mustard (usually French); also candied fruits in
mustard syrup, a sort of chutney, made in Cremona

mozzarella

soft white buffalo-milk cheese, a Neapolitan speciality
and one of the staple ingredients for *pizza* toppings;
also served fried and baked; *in carrozza* ('in a
carriage'), cheese savoury, fried cheese sandwich

muscoli

mussels

Napoli, napolitana
Naples, Neapolitan, with tomatoes and basil
nocchette
type of pasta made with egg (same as *farfalline*)
nocciola
hazelnut; *gelato di*, ice-cream
noce
nut, walnut; *di cocco*, coconut; *salsa di*, sauce, made with walnuts, oil, parsley and cream; *moscata*, nutmeg

oca
goose; *di Treviso*, cooked with celery
olio
oil; *di oliva*, olive
oliva
olive
olivette
slices of veal wrapped round ham, Parmesan and parsley
ombrina
Mediterranean fish (L. *Ombrina leccia*) with firm white flesh, similar to sea bass and usually served boiled (*in bianco*)
orata
large Mediterranean fish with silver scales, usually cooked with liquid (*al vino bianco*, for example)
orecchiette
('little ears'), type of pasta, small discs of pasta pushed into an ear-shape with the thumb; speciality of Apulia often served with a sauce containing broccoli and anchovies
origano
oregano
ortaggi
vegetable dishes
osso buco
('bone with a hole in it'), shin, or knuckle, of veal, cooked in wine and stock with tomatoes and served with rice; *alla milanese*, Milan-style (the dish originated in Milan)
ostriche
oysters (Taranto is famous for them); *alla veneziana* (Venice-style), with caviar

paesana, la
dessert of white raisins soaked in eau-de-vie (spirit, often fruit flavoured)

paesana, alla
peasant- or country-style; sauce made with bacon, Parmesan cheese and mushrooms

paeta
regional name for turkey in the Veneto

pagello
sea bream

paglia e fieno
('straw and hay'), yellow and green pasta served with a cream sauce (*alla ghiotta*, glutton-style)

palombacci
game pigeons

pancetta
bacon

pane
bread

panettone
large fruit cake, or spiced brioche, from Lombardy region, containing candied lemon peel and raisins or sultanas; a popular Christmas present

panforte
sugar cake made with honey, almonds, and candied melon, orange or lemon (speciality of Siena)

panini
bread rolls

panna
cream; *montata*, whipped; *alla parmigiana*, with Parmesan cheese

pannerone
a white version of gorgonzola, sometimes called *gorgonzola bianco*

pappa al pomodoro, la
Florentine soup made with bread, tomatoes and fresh basil

pappardelle
type of pasta, very broad noodles with crimped edges; *all'arrabbiata* ('angry'), with a sauce of tomatoes, chillis and bacon; *con la lepre*, Tuscan speciality, with a sauce of wild hare, wine and cheese

parmigiana, alla
sprinkled with Parmesan cheese (sometimes also denoting the presence of Parma ham); alternatively, may denote a dish from Parma

parmigiano
Parmesan cheese (hard, semi-sweet cheese from

province of Parma, though it in fact originated in the Enza valley, between Parma and Reggio); also called *grana* (meaning grain and denoting simply a hard, coarse-textured, crumbly type of cheese, of which real Parmesan is the finest)

parrozzo
a rich chocolate cake, speciality of the Abruzzi-Molise area

passato
purée; *di legume*, vegetable consommé; *di patate*, puréed potatoes

passatelli
dumplings; *alla bolognese* (Bologna-style), made with egg dough, cheese, breadcrumbs and beef marrow and cooked in consommé; *in brodo*, made with egg dough, cheese and spinach and cooked in consommé

pasta
(1) 'paste', pastry or dough of flour and water, used to make various types of noodles; generic name for various types and shapes of pasta; *asciutta* (dry), generic term for pasta served plain or with a sauce; *in brodo*, served as part of a soup; *e fagioli* (and beans), a thick Venetian soup; *frolla*, sweet short-crust pastry; *con sarde*, with sardines, Sicilian speciality; *all'uovo*, egg pasta, made with egg as well as flour and water: (2) cake

pastella
batter for deep frying

pasticceria
pastry

pasticciata
(Verona), meat stew; (Milan), a polenta dish baked *au gratin*

pasticciera, crema
custard cream made with sugar, eggs, milk, flour and lemon, used for dessert dishes

pasticcio
(1) pie, baked dish with pastry crust; *di anolini*, pie made with *pasta frolla* and *anolini*, once a special Sunday dish in Parma; *di maccheroni all'anziana* (Anzio pie), pie containing spaghetti and minced beef or veal, grated orange peel and cinamon, sometimes served with a meat sauce; *di maccheroni alla romana*, dessert dish, Roman-style, made with *rigatoni*, chicken livers, beef, mushrooms and gravy, *pasticciera* cream and *pasta frolla*: (2) pâté; *di fegato di maiale*, pork liver

pastiera
Neapolitan cake filled with cottage cheese and candied fruit; *napoletana*, Neapolitan Christmas speciality made of puff pastry with buttermilk and candied fruit

pastina
small pasta for soup

pastorella
soft cheese, similar to *bel paese*

patate
potatoes; *fritte*, fried; *al latte*, cooked in milk; *lesse*, boiled; *purée*, mashed

pavese
see *zuppa*

pecorino (romano)
Italy's oldest cheese, sharp, hard and white and made from sheep's milk; used in country districts instead of Parmesan; served with pears in Abruzzi region; *sardo*, Sardinian version

pelati
peeled plum tomatoes

penne
('feathers'), type of pasta cut in short pieces

peòci
mussels (Venetian name); *risotto di*, risotto with; *zuppa di*, soup

pepe
pepper; *nero*, black; *rosso*, red

peperata
sauce made of beef marrow, butter, breadcrumbs, Parmesan and stock, to accompany *bollito* or cooked hot or cold meat or poultry (speciality of Verona)

peperonata
stew made with sweet peppers and tomatoes

peperoni
sweet peppers, green (*verdi*), yellow (*gialli*) or red (*rossi*); *ripieni*, stuffed

peperoncini
dried or fresh hot red peppers

perciatelli
type of pasta, a thinner version of *maccaroncelli*

pere
pears; *al forno caramellata*, baked, and served with the caramelized juice; *ripiene*, stuffed, perhaps with gorgonzola cheese or with ground almonds and crystallized fruit

pernici
partridges; *arrosto*, roast, stuffed with bacon, ham,

mushrooms, juniper berries and the birds' liver; *in brodo*, cooked in broth containing vegetables and basil, served cold with a sauce made with lemon juice and parsley

pesce
fish

pesce persico
perch, found on the shores on the lake of Maggiore and served either grilled or fried in fillets or slices

pesce San Pietro
John Dory, celebrated in the Veneto region, cooked in various ways

pesce spada
swordfish, especially common in Sicily, served grilled, in slices

pesche
peaches; *ripiene*, stuffed (with macaroons, egg yolk, sugar and butter); *in vino bianco*, in white wine

pesto (alla genovese)
(Genoese) sauce for pasta based on olive oil, in which basil, pine nuts, garlic and both *pecorino* and Parmesan cheese have been steeped; *trenette col*, noodles with

pettirossi
robins

petto di pollo
chicken breast; *alla bolognese* (Bologna-style), fried, with Parmesan cheese and ham

petto di vitello
breast of veal; *arrotolato*, stuffed

pevarada
sauce made with lemon, oil and vinegar, garlic, anchovies, chicken livers, grated Parmesan cheese, pepper and ginger, served with game and roast meats

piccate
small, thin slices of fried veal, usually moistened with marsala and seasoned with lemon juice (same as *scaloppine*)

piccante
piquant

pignolata
Neapolitan pastry balls containing lemon and orange peel and dipped in honey

pignoli
pine nuts

pimiento
red sweet pepper

pincisgrassi

type of pasta, cooked in the oven with cheese and a sauce of meat, gravy and cream (Abruzzi-Molise area); see also *vincisgrassi*

piselli

peas; *al guanciale* (on a pillow), with fat pork and bacon; *alla toscana* (Tuscan-style), cooked in oil with garlic and bacon; see also *pisellini*

pisellini

tiny, very young peas, also called *piselli novelli*; *alla fiorentina* (Florence-style), sautéed with garlic, *prosciutto* and parsley; *al prosciutto*, cooked with onions and *prosciutto*, Roman speciality

pizza

large circular tart (literally 'pie') with a bread dough base, topped with mozzarella cheese, tomato and a wide variety of other ingredients, including capers, anchovies, marjoram, olives, mushrooms, salami, etc.; *bianco alla romana*, Roman-style, with mozzarella cheese and anchovies; *capricciosa*, topped with anchovies, tomatoes, mussels and mozzarella; *con cozze*, with mussels; *alla francescana*, topped with mushrooms, ham, cheese and tomatoes; *ai funghi*, with mushrooms; *margherita*, with tomatoes, mozzarella and Parmesan cheese; *alla liguria*, see *sardenara*; *alla marinara* (sailor-style), with garlic, tomatoes and olive oil; *napoletana* (Neapolitan), classic version with tomatoes, mozzarella, oregano and anchovies; *pasquale* (Easter), cake made with eggs, ricotta cheese and honey; *alla piemontese* (Piedmont-style), small, filled with tomatoes, peppers and anchovies and served as a starter; *quattro stagioni* ('four seasons'), with four types of topping, such as different cheeses, seafood and other variants on the usual ingredients; *rustica*, made with pastry, filled with a mixture of béchamel sauce, eggs, cheese, ham, salami and hard-boiled eggs, with a pastry top; *sardenara* (Ligurian), with olives, tomatoes, anchovies and onion; *siciliana* (Sicilian-style), with onions, tomato and salami

pizzaiola

style of sauce based on tomatoes, garlic and wild marjoram

pizzette

small pizzas

pizzichi

type of pasta made with egg (same as *farfalline*)

polenta
form of semolina made from maize, grown in northern Italy, yellow in colour and eaten either as an accompaniment to a meat dish, or seasoned with a sauce (meat, fish, tomato or mushroom, or combinations), or butter and cheese (e.g. Parmesan); a version of the latter is *polenta grassa* (rich), with layers of *fontina* and butter, either baked or grilled; *pasticciata*, pie, speciality of Milan; polenta is often served with little birds (*e osei*: a speciality of Bergamo and Brescia)

polipi
octopus

polipetti
small octopus

pollastro, pollastrino
spring chicken

pollo
chicken; *all'arrabbiata* ('angry'), braised with vegetables, including hot pepper and tomatoes, in white wine; *arrosto*, roast; *arrosto in tegame*, pot-roasted in white wine with garlic and rosemary; *alla cacciatora* (hunter's-style), braised in wine with mushrooms and tomatoes, sometimes also with green peppers; *alla diavola* ('devilled'), marinated in pepper, oil and lemon and grilled, ideally over charcoal; *finanziera di*, rich chicken mixture in pastry shell (Piedmontese speciality); *fritto*, fried, and served with lemon; *al latte*, cooked in milk; *al limone*, roast with lemon; *con olive*, stewed with vegetables and with olives added to the sauce; *petto di, alla bolognese* (Bologna-style)/*alla fiorentina* (Florence-style)/*alla senese* (Siena-style), breast of, with ham and cheese/fried in butter/with parsley and lemon; *in porchetta*, stuffed with ham and fennel and cooked in butter in the oven; *rollatini di petto di, e maiale*, filleted breast of, stuffed with pork; *tonnato*, served cold with tuna sauce; *in umido con cipolla*, stew with onion

polpette
meatballs or rissoles; *alla pizzaiola*, made with beef, cooked with tomatoes, mozzarella and anchovies

polpetti
sea strawberries, rosy-coloured baby squid (same as *fragoline di mare* and *moscardini*)

polpettine
small meatballs; *di baccalà*, made with salt cod; *alla fiorentina* (Florence-style) with artichokes; *di melanzane*, fried aubergine patties

polpettone
meat loaf, or large meat roll containing stuffing; *di tonno*, of tuna; *alla toscana* (Tuscan-style), braised in wine with dried mushrooms

pomodori
tomatoes; *al forno*, baked; *fritti*, fried; *coi gamberetti*, stuffed with prawns; *di mare*, stuffed with seafood; *minestra di*, soup; *alla siciliana* (Sicilian-style), baked, with anchovies, tuna and black olives; *col tonno*, stuffed with tuna; *zuppa crema di*, cream of, soup

pompelmo
grapefruit

porchetta
whole sucking pig, served spit-roasted in Umbria and the Marches

porri
leeks; *al burro e formaggio*, braised with Parmesan; *minestra di*, soup; *torta di, e patate*, and potato pie

potacchio
special stew or sauce; *anconetano* (from Ancona in the Marches), containing olive oil, white wine, garlic, tomatoes and herbs, served with all sorts of meat, poultry and fish

poveracce, poverasse
clams

prezzemolo
parsley

prosciutto
salted, air-cured, uncooked ham (not smoked), speciality of province of Parma; *di cinghiale*, of wild boar; *cotto*, cooked (boiled); *di San Daniele*, Venetian variety of *prosciutto*

provatura, provola
buffalo-milk cheese from Campania; *affumicata*, smoked, eaten with good olive oil and freshly ground pepper after the cheese's skin has been removed

provinciale
provincial, regional (cooking)

provolone
a piquant, semi-hard, creamy cheese that appears in various forms and sizes and may be made from either buffalo's or cow's milk

punta (di vitello arrosto)
breast (of veal, roasted)

punti
tips (e.g. of asparagus)

puntino, (cotto) al
  '(cooked) to the exact point', medium-rare (of steak)
purè, purea
  purée; *di patate*, mashed potatoes (with Parmesan
  cheese)
purée
  mashed, puréed

quadrucci
  ('little squares'), type of pasta made from cross-cut
  tagliatelle and used mainly in soups
quagliata
  curds, rennet
quaglie
  quails; *con piselli*, with peas, speciality of Capri
quagliette di vitello
  slices of veal wrapped round ham or other stuffing

radicchio
  radish; *rosso* (red), winter salad of Trieste area
rafano
  horseradish; *salsa verde al*, green sauce with
ragù (alla bolognese)
  meat and tomato sauce for pasta which originated in
  Bologna; *di funghi*, made with mushrooms; *alla
  pommarola*, a Neapolitan version made with tomatoes
rane
  frogs; *in brodo al riso*, dish made with frogs, onions,
  leeks and various herbs, with rice cooked in the liquid
  in which these were boiled; *dorate*, skinned, dipped in
  egg and fried in olive oil (*frittura di*), frogs' legs,
  treated in the same way), both specialities of
  Piedmont

rape
  turnips
rape rosse
  beetroots
ravioli
  type of pasta, squares stuffed with meat, vegetables
  (e.g. spinach) and cheese; *di spinaci e ricotta*,
  spinach and *ricotta* dumplings, also known as
  gnocchi del casentino
raviggiolo
  sheep's milk cheese made in Tuscany and Umbria
razza
  skate
ricotta
  soft, bland sheep's-milk cheese made from whey,
  akin to cottage cheese and much used in Emilia. It is
  eaten with sugar or cinnamon or salt and used a
  great deal in cooking
rigatoni
  type of pasta, ribbed, tubular macaroni, very popular
  in Florence served with veal *ragù*
ripieno
  filling, stuffing
riso
  rice; *arrosto alla genovese* (Genoa-style), timbale of
  sausage, vegetables and cheese, oven-baked; *in
  bianco*, boiled, also, in the Veneto, a soup (rice in
  consommé); *e ceci*, with chick peas, highly spiced
  and served in a tomato sauce; *al limone*, boiled, with
  lemon; *alla piemontese* (Piedmont-style), with white
  truffles
risi e bisi
  rice and peas (Venetian dish – sometimes listed
  under soups)
risotto
  rice cooked in butter with onions, with the addition
  of stock and white wine (*bianco*); *bianco* (in the
  Veneto) with fish; *alla certosina* (Carthusian-style),
  with prawns, mushrooms, peas and tomatoes; *di
  mare*, with seafood such as lobster and prawn; *alla
  marinara* (sailor-style), with clams; *alla milanese*,
  with saffron, which colours the dish deep yellow
  (classic accompaniment for *osso buco*); *di mitili*, with
  mussels; *alla paesana* (country-style), with early
  peas, courgettes and carrots; *di pesce, di pesse*, with
  fish; *primavera*, with spring vegetables; *alla sbirriglia*,
  with chicken cut into small pieces; *alla toscana*
  Tuscan-style), with pot-roast, mushrooms and

tomatoes; *alla veronese* (Verona-style), with ham, in mushroom sauce

ristretto

concentrated

robiola

soft, runny, white, full-flavoured cow's-milk cheese from Lombardy

robiolina

more powerful variety of *robiola*

rognoncini

kidneys; *trifolati*, sautéed, sliced lamb or veal kidneys

rolé

roll; *di manzo*, beef; *di vitello*, veal

rollatini

small rolls; *di vitello al pomodoro*, veal rolls with tomato sauce

romano

see *pecorino*

rosmarino

rosemary

rossa

red; *salsa*, sauce of onions, tomatoes and green peppers, with a little chilli, served warm with various meat dishes, including *bollito misto*

rotelle

type of pasta, usually served with *ragù*

sagnettine

type of pasta, otherwise known as *linguine*

salame

salami, spiced pork sausage (speciality of Bologna) of which many varieties exist, some strongly flavoured with garlic

salamoia

brine

sale

salt

salmi

stewed in wine and other ingredients (see *lepre*); classic Tuscan mode of cooking game

salmone

salmon

salsa

sauce; *genovese*, Genoese, made with veal, various vegetables, tomatoes and wine; *di pomodoro*, tomato, including also vegetables and meat; *di pomodoro al marsala*, with tomatoes, ham or bacon, garlic and Marsala; *piccante*, piquant, with red wine, oil, vinegar, herbs and garlic

salsiccia
fresh spiced sausage

saltato
sautéed

saltimbocca
('jump into the mouth'), a popular Roman dish consisting of slices of veal fillet rolled in ham, fried in butter, flavoured with sage and sprinkled with Marsala wine

salvia
sage

sangue, al
rare (of steak)

sanguinaccio
creamy dessert flavoured with chocolate (Neapolitan speciality)

saraghine
sardines (dialect word); *alla brace* (embers), grilled

sarde, sardelle
sardines (in Italy mainly fresh, not tinned); *in carpione*, fried and marinated with garlic and vegetables (Lombardy name: also known as *in saor* in the Veneto region and *a scapece* in Sicily), served without re-heating; *ripiene*, stuffed with bread and Parmesan cheese and fried

savoiarda
meat-and-fish salad, speciality of Monza, with calf's-head meat, boiled pork, tongue, tuna fish, anchovies, various pickles, capers, parsley and pickled yellow and red peppers

savoiardi
sponge fingers (used in *zuppa inglese*)

scaloppe, scaloppine
escalopes: small, thin slices (of veal, usually), often served moistened with Marsala and seasoned with lemon juice (see *piccate*)

scampi
scampi (shrimps); *fritti*, fried; *alla griglia*, grilled; *alle stecche*, on skewers; *in umido*, stewed

scarole
small, Batavian endives

scarpaccia
('big old shoe'), sort of large pizza made in Tuscany with courgettes, onion and Parmesan cheese

schie
  clams
scottiglia
  stew, usually incorporating pieces of bread
secco
  dry
sedano
  celery
selvaggina
  game
semolina
  cereal, the finely ground heart of the wheat
senapa
  mustard
sepolini
  squid
seppie
  cuttle-fish
sfinciuni
  double pizza, speciality of Palermo, with two layers
  of dough enclosing the stuffing, or *conzo* (e.g.
  tomato, onion and anchovy, or ricotta cheese and
  broccoli); *di San Vito*, with a stuffing of beef, ham,
  onion, breadcrumbs and *fontina* and ricotta cheese
sfinge (di San Giuseppe)
  Sicilian pastry flavoured with orange peel and made
  by monks
sfoglia
  flaky (of pastry)
sfogliatelle
  fan-shaped pastry filled with sweetened ricotta
  cheese and candied fruit, speciality of Naples
sformato
  mould; *di spinaci*, spinach
soffiato
  soufflé; *di gamberi*, prawn
soffrito
  a spicy base for soups, sauces and meat dishes
sogliola
  sole; *al marsala*, browned in butter and splashed
  with Marsala and fish broth; *alla parmigiana*, browned
  in butter and topped with Parmesan cheese
soppresse
  pork and beef salami, speciality of Verona
sorbetto
  sorbet
spada
  swordfish

spaghetti
type of pasta; *arrabbiata* ('angry'), with pimentos and tomatoes; *bolognese* (Bologna-style), with meat sauce (*ragù*) and Parmesan; *a cacio e pepe*, with *pecorino* and pepper; *alla carbonara*, with eggs, bacon (ideally *pancetta*) and Parmesan; *alla prestinara*, with only garlic and oil; *alla siciliana* (Sicilian-style), with aubergines and ricotta cheese

spalla di vitello brasata
shoulder of veal braised in white wine

speck
smoked raw ham, a version of *prosciutto* found in the Dolomite region

spigola
sea bass, usually served roasted or grilled (known as *branzino* on Adriatic coast)

spinaci
spinach; *sformato di*, mould

spuma
mousse

spumone
a frozen cream similar to ice-cream (speciality of Naples)

stecche, alle
on small sticks, skewered

stelline
('little stars'), type of miniature pasta for soups

stoccafisso
stockfish or salt cod (same as *baccalà*)

storione
sturgeon, fairly common on the Adriatic coast, usually served oven-roasted or cooked over charcoal

stracchino
soft cow's-milk cheese, similar to *taleggio*

stracci
type of pasta, irregular in shape, served with a sauce of tomato and pieces of mutton, also known as *carte da giuoco* (card-game)

stracciatella
('little rags'), soup made with meat broth, beaten eggs and Parmesan (Roman speciality)

stracotto
('overcooked', long-cooked), pot-roast (especially beef); *al Barolo*, beef braised in red wine; *alla fiorentina*, Florentine beef stew cooked in chianti

strangolapreti, strangolaprieviti
('priest-stranglers'), type of pasta, dumplings containing cheese, egg and pieces of bacon; also known as *gnocchetti cacio e ova*

stufato
('smothered'), stew; *manzo, al vino rosso*, beef, in red wine; *di manzo alla genovese*, Genoese beef, with vegetables and white wine

stufatino
stew; *alla romana*, Roman-style, made with beef, bacon, marjoram and red wine

succutundu
Sardinian dish, a highly concentrated *bouillon* containing balls of semolina

suffli
soufflé: light, frothy, baked egg dish

sugo
sauce (particularly for pasta), juice; *di carne*, meat sauce, incorporating onion, carrot, celery, dried mushrooms and wine; *di pomodoro*, tomato juice

supplì
rice croquettes, also containing *mortadella* sausage (or ham) and cheese; *al telefono*, 'telephone croquettes', containing buffalo-milk cheese (*provatura* or *mozzarella*) that hangs down like telephone wires when the croquette is bitten

tacchino
turkey; *arrosto ripieno*, roast, and stuffed with its own liver, veal, chestnuts, Parmesan cheese and prunes; *stufato al vino bianco*, braised, in white wine

taccozzelle
type of pasta, rectangular in shape, served with cottage cheese and tomato sauce

tagliarini
alternative name for *tagliolini*

tagliatelle
type of pasta cut into thin strips (ribbon egg noodles); *alla bolognese* or *al ragù*, served with special meat sauce devised in Bologna; *al pesto*, with *pesto* sauce; *al ragù*, same as *alla bolognese*

tagliolini
type of pasta, thinner version of *tagliatelle*

taleggio
mild, creamy cow's-milk cheese from Lombardy

taleggino
stronger variety of *taleggio*

tartufi
truffles; *bianchi*, white; *di mare*, sea, served raw; *neri*, black

te
tea

telline
clams (Florentine name) or mussels

tomini del talucco
a goat's-milk cheese made in Piedmont, at Pinado

tonnarelle
type of pasta, cut thin; *alla paesana* (country-style), served with a *ragù* containing mushrooms and bacon

tonnellini
type of pasta, very fine homemade egg noodle; *con funghi e piselli*, with mushrooms and peas

tonno
tuna or tunny fish; *salsa di*, hot sauce containing also parsley and butter

topinambur
Jerusalem artichokes; *gratinati*, gratinée, with a Parmesan topping; *insalata di, e spinaci*, and spinach salad; *trifolati*, sautéed

tordi
thrushes

torrone
nougat, speciality of Cremona; *molle*, soft, a sweet made with cocoa, sugar, butter, eggs, plain biscuits and ground almonds

torta
(sweet) tart, flan, cake, pie; *pasqualina*, elaborate (Genoese) Easter pie made with leeks or artichokes, curds, grated cheese, milk, olive oil and eggs in a puff-pastry case; *di riso*, sweet rice cake, Easter speciality of Bologna

tortellini
type of pasta, resembling tiny hats and stuffed with a pork, egg, cheese and spice mixture, served either with a *ragù* or in a soup

tortelloni
type of pasta, large squares usually served stuffed with Swiss chard or spinach; *di biete*, stuffed with Swiss chard; *al burro e formaggio*, cooked with butter and Parmesan

tortiglione
almond cakes

tortiglioni
type of pasta, similar to the corkscrew-shaped *fusilli*

tortino di carciofi
eggs with artichokes, Florentine speciality

totani
long-bodied squid; *al prezzemole*, with parsley

trenette
type of pasta, Genoa's name for thin ribbon noodles, same as *tagliolini*; see also *pesto*

tremezzini
sandwiches

triglie
red mullet, speciality of Livorno; *gravide*, 'pregnant', stuffed with a mixture of *prosciutto* and parsley; *alla livornese* (Livorno-style), with tomato sauce

trionfo di gola
('triumph of the palate'), acclaimed Sicilian sweet made by monks to a secret recipe

trippa
tripe; *alla fiorentina* (Florence-style), with tomato sauce and Parmesan cheese; *alla parmigiana*, fried served with melted Parmesan cheese; *alla romana* (Roman-style), braised, with tomatoes, white wine, carrot, garlic and herbs

trota
trout; *in bianco*, boiled; *ai ferri*, grilled; *fritta*, fried; *marinata all'arancio*, marinated with orange and served cold

tubetti
type of pasta, same as *ditalini*

tufoli
type of pasta, giant stuffed macaroni tubes

ubriaco
 'drunken' (usually, cooked in wine)
uccelletti
 small birds, such as thrushes, larks, blackbirds, robins and bullfinches, served roasted or grilled, with *polenta* (in northern Italy), *migliaccio* and/or rice; *scappati* ('escaped'), slices of veal wrapped round ham or other stuffing
uova
 egg; *alla cocca*, boiled; *alla fiorentina* (Florence-style), oven-baked dish of poached eggs on buttered spinach; *sode in salsa verde*, hard-boiled, with green sauce
uva
 grapes; *nera*, black
uva spina
 gooseberry

valdostana
 in the style of the Val d'Aosta
valligiana, alla
 in the style of the valley (local version)
vaniglia
 vanilla
ventresca
 tuna fish
verde
 green (usually denoting spinach); *salsa*, sauce, made with parsley, capers and anchovies, classic accompaniment for *bollito misto* and various fish and meat dishes
verdure
 vegetables or greens
vermicelli
 type of pasta, very fine spaghetti used in soups

verza

savoy cabbage

vincisgrassi

name used in the Marches, where it originated, for the baked pasta dish *pincisgrassi*

vitello

veal; *tonnato*, sliced with tuna sauce, a classic cold dish

vongole

shellfish, cockles or clams (southern Italian name)

zabaglione, zabaione

egg and Marsala sauce; also frothy dessert dish (containing sugar in addition), served warm in glasses

zafferano

saffron

zampa

(calf's) leg

zamponi

pigs' trotters, a speciality of Modena, which are stuffed with seasoned pork, boiled for several hours and served, thickly sliced, with *salsa verde* or mustard

zemino

see *zimino*

zeppole

sweet made of honey, dried figs, almonds and other nuts, speciality of the Abruzzi-Molise region; *alla napoletana* (Naples-style), brandy-flavoured fritters; *di San Giuseppe*, cinnamon-flavoured fritters, shaped like a ring doughnut, sold from street stalls (speciality for St Joseph's Day)

zimino

fish stew; see *lumache*

ziti

type of pasta, large tubes of macaroni

zucca

pumpkin; *cappellacci di*, pasta filled with (speciality of Ferrara)

zucchine/zucchini

courgettes, baby marrows; *frittata di*, omelette with courgettes; *fritte*, fried battered slices; *della nonna* (grandmother's), fried in oil with the addition of beaten egg and grated Parmesan

zuccotto
rich Florentine dessert made with sponge cake, cocoa, chocolate, liqueur and spirits

zuppa
soup; *alla certosina* (Carthusian-style), breaded vegetable; *di cozze*, mussel; *di datteri*, with shellfish (sea dates, found off the Genoese coast); *di frutti di mare*, seafood; *alla genovese*, fish; *di granchi*, crab; *inglese* (see below); *di lenticchie*, lentil; *di mitili*, mussel; *alla pavese* (Pavia-style), hot broth poured over eggs on slices of toast; *di peòci*, Venetian mussel; *di pesce*, fish; *di pomodoro*, tomato; *primavera*, spring vegetable; *reale*, royal, with separate egg yolks and whites (Abruzzi speciality); *di vercolore*, green soup, with vegetables, herbs and watercress; *di verdure*, vegetable; *di vongole*, clam

zuppa inglese
trifle, decorated with whipped cream and crystallized fruit

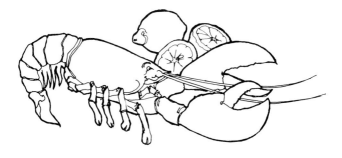

Italian Wines

Italy produces a greater amount of wine than any other country in the world. Italian wines have long found favour with wine lovers, and in recent years with the prices rocketing for Bordeaux and Burgundy, they have made even greater inroads into the market. Few wines reach the very highest quality but, as with Spain, there are a number of excellently priced and produced wines that merit attention. As for the traveller, motoring around the provinces, his will be a journey of discovery, for the variety of wines to sample in Italy is truly enormous.

Veneto

A wine area of note, producing large quantities of delicious wine, especially Valpolicella, Bardolino and the excellent whites of Soave.

Lombardy

Wines of quality are to be found here, in particular the Sassella and Grumello. Also worth noting are the wines from Freccirossa, a privately owned regulated area, producing an excellent dry white, a delicious rosé and a first class red.

Piemonte

The great wine growing district of Italy, with many of her finest and most prestigious wines, dependent for their quality on the Nebbiolo grape. Barolo, Barberesco, Barbera and Gattinara are the most famous wines, big-flavoured, full-bodied wines with good aging qualities, high in alcohol.

Emilia-Romagna

This is hearty country, with a gastronomy based on the stomach rather than the senses. The wines of the area are hardly distinguished, although there are one or two notable exceptions, in particular the Sangiovese. Good whites are made as well as the exceptionally individualistic Lambrusco – loved by many, loathed by more.

Tuscany

Italy's most famous export, Chianti, is to be found here amongst the Tuscan hills. The quality of Chianti seems to have dropped in recent years as the market has demanded more and more in volume to satisfy the world's pizza parlours and trattorias. There are always exceptions, especially from the houses of Antinori, Pagliaresi, Ricasoli, Ruffino amongst others. The wines of Brunello di Montalcino, from near Siena, fetch high prices not always matched by quality – the wines from the house of Biondi-Santi are an exception.

Lazio

The area which encroaches right to the outskirts of Rome can boast wines of real quality, in particular the dessert wines from Castelli Romani – late-gathered and delicious – Frascati and Est! Est! Est!, whose claim to fame lies with its name rather than its vinous qualities.

Sicily

From Sicily comes the dessert wine of Marsala, apparent in much of Italy's cuisine, it also has an important place on the wine list. A fortified wine, not unlike Madeira, which improves considerably with age.